asking
questions

IAN MACKAY

Second edition

Management Shapers is a comprehensive series covering all the crucial management skill areas. Each book includes the key issues, helpful starting points and practical advice in a concise and lively style. Together, they form an accessible library reflecting current best practice – ideal for study or quick reference.

Other titles in the series:

The Institute of Personnel and Development is the leading publisher of books and reports for personnel and training professionals, students, and all those concerned with the effective management and development of people at work. For full details of all our titles please contact the Publishing Department:

tel. 0181-263 3387
fax 0181-263 3850
e-mail publish@ipd.co.uk

The catalogue of all IPD titles can be viewed on the IPD website:
http://www.ipd.co.uk

asking
questions

IAN MACKAY

Second edition
revised and updated by
Krystyna Weinstein

INSTITUTE OF PERSONNEL AND DEVELOPMENT

First published 1980 by the British Association for Commercial and
Industrial Education, entitled *A Guide to Asking Questions*.
Second edition in the *Training Extras* series 1995
Reprinted 1997
First published in the *Management Shapers* series in 1998

Design by Curve
Typesetting by Paperweight
Printed in Great Britain by
The Guernsey Press, Channel Islands

British Library Cataloguing in Publication Data
A catalogue record for this book is available from the
British Library

ISBN
0-85292-768-1

The views expressed in this book are the author's own and
may not necessarily reflect those of the IPD.

**INSTITUTE OF PERSONNEL
AND DEVELOPMENT**

IPD House, Camp Road, London SW19 4UX
Tel.: 0181 971 9000 Fax: 0181 263 3333
Registered office as above. Registered Charity No. 1038333.
A company limited by guarantee. Registered in England No. 2931892.

contents

introduction

Most people spend a large part of their lives asking and answering questions. From the broad-based 'How are you?' right across the spectrum to the (hopefully rare!) ordeal of highly specific cross-examination in courts of law, we cannot escape this basic aspect of our existence. Yet few people are really aware of the different types of question available to them. Nor are they aware what answers will result from the questions they do ask.

A moment's reflection shows that such 'question-askers' work in a very wide range of occupations: the police officer investigating a traffic accident or a crime; the doctor exploring the causes of a patient's ill-health; the social worker assessing the effect of domestic problems with a member of the household; the probation officer analysing an adolescent's behaviour with a parent; the manager investigating work problems with colleagues, or evaluating a candidate's suitability for employment; the counsellor assisting a client; the union official negotiating on behalf of his members; even the teacher helping students to learn by posing questions. Their success depends on asking the right questions and accurately assessing the responses in order to make the right decisions.

So, all of us ask questions. Questions are the stuff of conversation; they are part of our everyday work and play, our study and our leisure. We ask them for a variety of reasons:

- to gain more information
- to open up a discussion or debate
- to seek clarification
- to get someone's co-operation
- to involve and motivate others
- to help people reflect and learn.

We may also, of course, ask questions to show how clever we are and to show up others' ignorance.

Questions can be divided into three categories: the open, the closed, and the counter-productive. Open ones encourage others to open out; closed ones usually require monosyllabic responses from a respondent, and place the onus of 'working' on the questioner. Counter-productive questions are just that – unhelpful questions.

Asking questions isn't simply a matter of the words, however. The tone of voice in which they are asked is also important. Some questions need to be asked in a 'supportive' way, others in a more 'challenging' way. Some people respond to challenge, others withdraw. When to use each is often up to the discretion of the person posing the questions.

We may also 'ask' questions in non-verbal ways, or make statements that act as pseudo-questions or prompts for the speaker to continue. We may, of course, ask questions to which we don't want replies – we provide them ourselves! Worse still, we don't wait for the response but interrupt the speaker. The following pages describe each of these aspects of questioning in greater detail.

The important thing to remember, however, is that questioning is not simply a skill that only interviewers or assessors need to have. Asking good questions is something that everyone who works with others should be able to do – to tap into and use their knowledge and insights, to discuss and debate with colleagues, to find out things – ultimately to learn.

By asking questions we are, in the words of Reg Revans, admitting to our own ignorance. And we learn only if we admit to that ignorance.

There is a skill in asking the 'right' questions – ones that elicit what we are seeking. Let me give one simple example of this. Asking someone 'why' they have done something may not give us the response we hope to get. If I ask, 'Why have you come on this course?', the person I have asked may respond in a number of ways: 'Because my boss sent me';

'Because I wanted to learn about X.' But if I have asked the question in the hope of finding out what the respondent hoped to get from coming on the course, I will have failed, because I didn't ask the 'right' question. It was too vague. I should have asked, 'What do you hope to get from this course?'

This booklet addresses therefore the issue of the types of question we need to ask, and the form in which to ask them in order to gain the responses we are seeking. The 'right' form of questions also helps our respondents to use their brains. This is one of the more exciting uses of questions: to show others that they have the answers within themselves!

The paradox is, of course, that the minute the question has been asked, the questioner becomes the listener! So a good questioner has also to be a good listener. They are two sides of the same coin. (See *Listening Skills* by the same author in this series.)

1 open questioning

Open questions – ones that encourage the other person to speak, and utter more than monosyllables – are valuable for several reasons. Obviously they give the questioner more information, greater insights, and more understanding, either of the other person or the topic around which the questions are revolving.

However, much of their value is also for the respondent. Being asked 'good' questions, maybe by colleagues or a manager, means we have to think more deeply, possibly, about some issue we have not thought of before or have avoided. Being asked questions – if they are asked in the right spirit – is also highly motivating. A manager who asks members of staff what they think should be done about an issue, instead of issuing instructions, will have a more motivated workforce. Asking for others' opinions (see 'Opinion-seeking questions' below) and being prepared to listen to the response (a vital element) means they will feel their opinions on ideas are valued.

Another interesting result of having to respond to questions – again, if asked in the right spirit – is that they force the respondent to think, and in that process he or she often finds within themselves ideas, thoughts, or knowledge they never suspected they had!

But knowing how to phrase questions effectively isn't sufficient. The questioner has also to be able to interpret the answers, if only to know how to follow on – possibly with further questions. This applies as much to managers asking their staff questions as it does to professional interviewers or assessors.

Accurate interpretation is of prime importance, particularly throughout an interview. Correct assessment of verbal facility, sequence of ideas, development of the theme etc together with a real appreciation of the emotional undertones of the response will assist the interviewer in deciding the direction of subsequent discussion. But how can this be done? It is one thing to talk about such assessment, quite another to put it into practice. Whether the assessment is accurate will depend on how effectively the replies are analysed. This means not only listening (literally) to what is being said but also listening 'between the lines'. A truly effective analysis will be conducted at a number of different levels and will be based on the answers to the following questions:

- What is the respondent actually saying?

- What do they *seem* to be trying to communicate?

- What can be inferred from the way they communicate and the words they use?

- What do they convey by their whole manner of approach to the subject?

It should also be remembered during an interview that it is not what the interviewer actually says which is all important, but the interpretation given to his statements by the respondent. For this reason a poorly phrased open question may well result in the respondent becoming at best hesitant or at worst evasive, because the wording of the question has left in doubt what is expected. This doubt may also produce tension.

The major disadvantage of using open questions is that by encouraging the respondent to talk freely the interviewer may let the respondent talk too much. If this does happen then it is the interviewer who must guide the discussion smoothly back towards its purpose.

Open questions fall into two categories: those involving either 'active' or the more 'passive' forms of questioning (see the table on page 8). Each can be useful for an interviewer, a manager, or indeed anyone!

Active questioning

Active questioning could be either to establish contact or to 'probe'.

Contact questions

First in this category are the gentle forms of 'contact' questions. As the name implies, they are designed to establish the first step in a relationship and put people at ease. They help to establish a friendly atmosphere and form the basis

---

Open questions

Active questioning

◉ Contact questions — to establish rapport
▣ Probing questions — to seek further information

   – simple interrogative — to encourage the person being questioned to think and find solutions themselves

   – comparative — to explore in detail
   – extensions and precision — to challenge
   – opinion-seeking ⎫
   – hypothetical ⎭ — to test knowledge/thinking

   – reflection ⎫
   – summary ⎭ — to draw threads together/ test understanding

---

Passive questioning

◉ non-verbal encouragement ⎫
▣ supportive comments/ link questions ⎪ — to encourage, to give space and time, to show interest, to draw out
△ key work repetition ⎬
◉ mirror questions ⎪
◉ pause ⎭

---

for subsequent discussions. They occur at the beginnings of meetings when strangers meet, or when a new person comes to be interviewed for a job. For instance, an interviewer might start with something like: 'I see from your background that you come from Winchester. That gives us something in common because I was born and bred there. I've got fond memories of the place but hear there have been some changes recently …?' Or they might ask: 'I hope you didn't have any difficulty in finding us today?' Another possibility might be: 'How would you describe yourself to someone who doesn't know you?' (ie 'Tell me something about yourself.')

Such questions should not be overused, however, because the respondent will begin to wonder when the interview proper will begin, and this may make him feel edgy. But because the initial stages of most interviews can feel threatening, every effort should be made to put the interviewee at ease with such general questions.

Even the beginning of meetings attended by a group of people, or a first encounter of the day with a colleague, may also be eased by what is often described as 'small talk'. So, other contact questions that play a similar role might include:

- 'How have you been since we last met?'
- 'I don't think we've met before?'
- 'Did you have a good holiday/weekend?'
- 'I believe you've just joined us?'

Some contact questions often don't require a real response eg 'Nice day, isn't it?' They are simply one person making contact with another.

Probing questions

There are several varieties of probing questions. What may prompt them is an interviewer seeking information about an interviewee. However, such questions arise all the time in many everyday instances, eg when someone asks a colleague or manager for help, saying, 'I don't know how to ...', or asking, 'What do you think I should do about ...?' Instead of piling in with advice, a much more powerful way is to begin to ask that person questions that will help *them* to understand the issue more fully and even come up with insights and solutions. This is the route to creating motivated staff and people with confidence, ready to take on responsibilities.

Probing questions are designed to search for information in much greater depth. Sometimes called 'follow-up' or 'focusing' questions, their main object is to get beyond the (possibly) superficial replies and investigate in more detail. Of course, this does not mean that probing should be carried out like an interrogation. If the questioner assumes the role of insensitive interrogator such an attitude will certainly offend and embarrass the respondent, and at worst provoke a positively hostile reaction.

An interviewer may, for instance, need to explore some aspects of background or personality which the respondent would prefer to conceal. Throughout the interview the atmosphere should be one of calm, friendly enquiry. The establishment of such an atmosphere through judicious use of open questions will pave the way for a more detailed investigation without the probe questions seeming to be intrusive. As in many other social situations, *what* is said may be rather less important than *how* it is said.

Probing requires sympathy and careful listening to be really effective. It is not a skill that can be developed overnight but one that must be tested and refined as a result of experience.

The simple interrogative. The simple interrogative is a question form well known to parents of small children. A child very quickly learns that the most effective way of prolonging a discussion is to ask the question, 'Why?' No matter what explanation is offered by the adult this is immediately countered with another 'Why?' Whilst it may extend the child's education, the results depend to a great extent on the adult's knowledge of the subject and his ability with words. In any event, and as any parent will readily admit, it is very wearing!

'Why?' and 'Why not?' are extremely useful probes for a questioner, but again they must be used sensitively. Although the questioner is unlikely to be faced with the frustrated response of 'Because I say so!', such an approach can sound rather threatening to a respondent, and overuse has the effect of turning the conversation into an interrogation. However, there will be occasions when the questioner may wish to probe deeper into the reasons for a particular response. She must then soften the effect of a bald 'Why?' by asking more helpful questions – ones that begin to peel away layers, rather like removing the skin of an onion!

'Why did you say that?'

'I'm interested in your reasons for saying that ...'

'What, particularly, makes you say that?'

'How did you think that would ...?'

The use of such phrases, when further softened by an open, non-aggressive facial expression and tone of voice, will help to maintain the spirit of friendly enquiry built up previously.

Comparative questions. Comparative questions are extremely useful in a variety of situations to enable the questioner not only to make evaluation on a 'before and after' basis, but also to make a respondent think.

'What has the situation been like for you since ... happened?'

'We introduced the new procedure on the 14th. How efficient has the order system been since then?'

'How much did that experience alter your view of life?'

'To what extent did attendance at that course change your attitude to your job?'

'How do you feel now that the treatment is complete compared with how you felt previously?'

'How much has your attitude towards him changed now that you know the facts of the situation?'

'What difference have the last twelve months made to her skill in handling people?'

'To what extent has the new filing system improved administration in the department?'

'What changes have you noticed in your approach to counselling since we had that last session?'

Development and ordering of ideas, fluency in language, and ability to learn from experience as expressed in changes in opinions and attitudes are amongst the factors which may be assessed using this question form.

For instance, throughout a selection interview evidence is being sought to assess the candidate's suitability for the job in question. Comparative data can provide a very useful base for subsequent analysis, for example:

'How do your responsibilities now compare with those in your last job?'

'How does your own performance as a manager now compare with that of the best boss you've ever had?'

'What is your attitude now towards staff specialists compared with what it was when you were one yourself?'

Hypothetical questions. Such questions, which tend to be phrased in terms of 'What would you do if ...?' and 'How would you feel if ...?, give the person being asked the opportunity to put their knowledge, experience, and social skills to the test.

An example from an interview for a managerial appointment illustrates the point:

'Let's assume that you have been appointed to this post. What would you do if you found another manager criticising one of your own staff to his face?'

Hypothetical questions should not be used extensively in a selection interview, even though they are used to a greater extent in psycho-therapeutic counselling sessions, when they are sometimes known as 'fantasy' questions. In this situation, the questions tend to take the following form:

'If you had unlimited resources ...?'

'If you were suddenly to become ...?'

However, the hypothetical question can be used to great effect in work-related situations. It stimulates the respondent to challenge assumptions and encourages the adoption of an analytical approach to problem-solving. The hypothetical question in this situation can be summed up in two words: 'What if ...?' For example:

'What if we looked at the problem in this way?'

'What if Sales were to get involved at an earlier stage?'

'What if there was a weekly up-date?'

'What if they were shown the job first before deciding?'

'What if the equipment was bought rather than hired?'

'What if the payment period was extended?'

In each case the questioner is seeking a judgement from the respondent by saying (in effect), 'What do you think would happen if ...?' or 'What do you think the situation would be if ...?' The use of this type of question, when mixed with simple interrogative and other probes, will help to prompt the respondent towards a reasoned analysis.

Another variation of the hypothetical question is what may be called the 'role-exchange' question. For example:

'If you were in my position, what would you do?'

The 'role-exchange' can be useful in a number of different interview situations to get the respondent to 'see' the 'problem' from another point of view. If it is used unwisely, however, control of the interview may be lost. This is because the question can appear to be nothing more than a plea for understanding or even for a decision with which the interviewer can then agree.

Extension and precision questions. Careful listening to a response may perhaps show inconsistencies or pointers to topics which require further clarification or explanation. The extension (or reinforcement) question is designed to prompt a fuller answer. We're back to removing the layers of onion skin! Examples of this approach are:

'How do you mean?'

'How do you know?'

'How would you put that idea into action?'

'How about the other side of the question?'

'How else could this be achieved?'

'How can you be sure?'

'What are you thinking of specifically?'

'What makes you say that?'

'What particularly did you have in mind?'

'What other possible courses of action are there?'

'What happened to make you feel like that?'

'What do you mean when you say …?'

All the questions above should be a positive help in prompting the respondent to add to what they have already said.

There are other questions – precision questions – which are equally valuable and powerful when applied in everyday work situations:

'Can you enlarge on that?'

'Could you be a little more precise?'

'Have you any other ideas on this point?'

'Could you clarify that last point for me?'

'I wonder if you would develop that a little further?'

'Can you explain that in a little more detail?'

'Can you tell me a little more about that?'

Used in interviews, however, these questions might produce an extended answer, particularly with a forthcoming respondent. However, take the first question on the list:

'Can you enlarge on that?'

The answer might come back, 'Well, yes ... there is one thing I'd like to add. Let me explain. Now ... etc.' If the question provokes this kind of response then the questioner will have achieved his purpose. On the other hand, if the answer is a tart 'No, I've nothing to add to what I've just said', then the questioner will have failed. The use of a neutral 'How do you mean?' would have prevented this failure. Consider another example:

'Could you be a little more precise?'

This particular question might well produce the reluctant response, 'No ..., I don't think so', and it would require further questions to pull the interview back towards its purpose. The same aim could have been achieved more cleanly and more positively by the use of a genuine extension question such as, 'What are you thinking of specifically?'

Opinion-seeking questions. The purpose of using an opinion-seeking question is to explore a respondent's opinion or attitudes. Such questions give free rein to the respondent to outline his thoughts on a particular topic in as much depth as he wishes. So, for instance:

'How do you feel about ...?'

'What do you think about ...?'

'What are your views on ...?'

If the questioner then wants to investigate the respondent's views in rather more detail he could use a probing question. Such a probe is no more than a follow-up to the initial opinion-seeking question. It serves to focus the respondent's attention on a particular aspect of the broader topic previously aired. In other words, the probe is the equivalent of a supplementary question in Parliament. But instead of searching only for additional *facts*, as many supplementary questions are designed to do, the probe is searching exclusively for more detailed *opinions* and indications of more deep-seated *attitudes*.

A probe is a very useful question form in a wide variety of interview situations where the aim is to probe beyond the superficial, or possibly even evasive, responses to opinion-seeking questions, and establish the depth of conviction, degree of knowledge, or level of understanding.

In each of the following examples the first question in the series is an opinion-seeking question which is open and indirect. It is followed by a number of probes. These follow-up questions focus attention on particular areas within the broad topic. They are not closed questions because they still cannot be answered by a simple 'yes' or 'no', or by a short factual answer.

Example 1:
(a) 'How do you feel about the recent growth of legislation in the employment field?'

(b) 'To what extent do you believe employees' rights in employment should be further defined by law?'

(c) 'How far would you say the spirit of the anti-discrimination laws is being observed?'

(d) 'Just how much further do you think these particular laws are likely to be extended in the future?

Example 2:

(a) 'It has been said that more effort must be devoted to conserving our energy resources. What do you think about it?'

(b) 'How do you think other forms of energy might be exploited?'

(c) 'To what degree should governments co-operate on developing an international approach to energy conservation?'

(d) 'In what particular ways should the public be persuaded to become more energy-conscious?'

In each of these examples the use of qualifying phrases is worth noting. Phrases like:

'To what extent do you feel ...?'

'Just how far do you think ...?'

'In what ways ...?'

'Just how much ...?'

'To what degree ...?'

are all indications that the questioner is seeking an evaluation of the situation from the respondent.

Such phrases not only prompt evaluation: they are also useful guides to the degree of emotion involved. Accurate assessment of the depth of feeling transmitted by the tone of voice and other non-verbal indicators can act as a signpost for further questions. This may be particularly useful in a variety of situations such as negotiating or bargaining encounters, and in television interviews with politicians. Skilled questioners can often persuade (even entice) some politicians to commit themselves rather more than they had intended by an adroit mixing of opinion-seeking, simple interrogative, and extension and precision probes.

Opinion-seeking questions asked of staff by a manager, and related to everyday work situations, are one of the more powerful ways of making staff gain a sense of involvement in their work and feel their opinions are valued. After all, they are the ones who often know most about those everyday situations, and have plenty of ideas. Motivation – that elusive quality sought at work – often results from involving staff by this simple means of asking questions!

The reflection. Although this particular question is probably one of the most difficult to put into words effectively, it is extremely useful for exploring attitudes and opinions in detail. However, the reflection depends to a great extent on empathy – the difficult task of being able to put yourself in the position of the other person and truly understand what they are saying. To be effective in the use of the reflection, the questioner needs to listen carefully to what is being said, interpret it accurately, and respond accordingly.

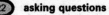

The most usual form of reflection is phrased as a statement rather than as an identifiable question. It tends to begin with phrases like:

'You feel that …?'

'It seems to you that …?'

These words indicate to the respondent that the interviewer is interpreting the emotional undertones of what is being said. The statement should never try to guess at feelings. They should always interpret accurately, because a poor interpretation may provoke a hostile reaction – 'No, I don't feel that way at all!'

Using the reflection is a little like tuning a radio. There will be considerable interference from other stations until the operator 'homes in' on just the right frequency, at which point the transmission will be heard clearly. This is just what the questioner is doing when making a reflective statement – 'homing in' on the response, getting a clear message of the feelings behind the words, rather than merely hearing the words themselves, and then reflecting this message back to the respondent. The questioner, by accurate interpretation of what is being said, is indicating that they fully appreciate the implications of the response.

A reflective statement may strike a barely audible chord with the respondent, who might need a few moments to think about its implications. A pause is often necessary to allow the respondent to order their thoughts. If the questioner interrupts with a comment or a further question, it may prevent the respondent voicing those thoughts (see The Pause, pages 32–4).

The questioner should maintain a neutral stance ie the reflection used should express the viewpoint 'I'm with you and understand what you're saying' rather than 'I'm in complete agreement with you.' Detachment is the key word, and any indication of approval or disapproval should be avoided.

However, if reflective statements are used effectively to probe a respondent's feelings they can yield much valuable information which might otherwise be missed.

Illustrations (from a variety of situations) of responses followed by reflective statements are shown below.

'Everybody says it'll be all right. … I suppose they know what they're talking about. I mean … they do, don't they?'

'You have your doubts?'

'… although I wonder if I might not get fed up with just typing all day.'

'You'd feel happier with something rather more demanding?'

'… and what's more, she's always picking on me and telling me off about everything I do. It never happens with the others.'

'You sense it's something personal?'

'My husband's people always ignore me when we're round at their place. It's just as if they wished we'd never met. It's so embarrassing … I know he appreciates how I feel and I'm sure he really wants to have it out with them but … Oh, I don't know. …'

'You feel it's a question of divided loyalties?'

'… and whenever I attend that meeting I always get the feeling that they're banding together to put me down. They reject everything I say, I mean … we're all working for the same organisation, aren't we?'

'You consider they're being unreasonable?'

'… so on top of all that, the costings are up the creek. Of course it's not Accounts' fault. It's that idiot in the office – spends his time in a dream – he's hopeless, can't get anything right!'

'You reckon they ought to get somebody else to do the job?'

'… anyway, he never normally buys me anything special. When the flowers arrived I was really surprised … it made my day.'

'You were touched by this gesture?'

A word of warning about using reflective statements: not only must the underlying emotions be accurately identified but the statement itself must be phrased in such a way that it invites further comment.

For example, the last two statements above might produce the following comments.

'You reckon they ought to get somebody else to do that job?' (statement)

'Too right ... and the sooner the better!' (response)

'You were touched by this gesture?' (statement)

'... I certainly was.' (response)

In both cases the respondent is indicating some unwillingness to develop the topic further. Any reflective statement might produce such a closed response. Only careful listening and accurate assessment of what has gone before will show whether its use is indicated or whether a different kind of probe should be used.

Summary questions. Summary questions, like reflective statements, are concerned with interpreting a response, but rather than reflecting emotional content they concentrate on factual content. Every interview, in particular, falls into a number of sections, and once the interviewer has gained sufficient information within a given section he must then move on to explore other areas. However, many novice interviewers are either unable to stop a garrulous respondent or are unsure of how to change direction smoothly without seeming too abrupt.

Summary questions can be used to review briefly, to summarise, to check the interviewer's understanding of the facts, or even to clarify the respondent's own thoughts. This is why they are sometimes called 'confirming' or 'crystallising' questions. Questions like:

'As I understand it ...?'

'If I've got it right ...?'

'So what you're saying is ...?'

are examples of this particular approach.

These questions can be extremely useful in a wide variety of interviewing situations. In a selection interview, for instance, the questioner may wish to confirm the reasons for a somewhat mediocre school record by saying something like: '... so what you're saying is that with more positive help from the staff and with greater effort on your part your results would have been much better?'

Again, in a progress interview, the manager may wish to crystallise for his own benefit the reasons for the partial failure of a particular exercise. Following discussion of the topic he might summarise by saying:

'As I understand it then, the main thing that went wrong was … and you're saying it could have been avoided by …. So next time you reckon we've got to make sure that …. Is that right?'

The same approach is appropriate in other situations where clarification is required. For example, a police officer arriving at the scene of an accident will probably ask some factual questions initially and may then follow up with the question, 'What happened?' Having listened to the response, a summary will ensure that he has understood what has been said:

'You were driving at about 25 mph when an animal, you're not sure what, ran in front of you. You swerved and then hit the lamp-post. Is that right?'

The other main use of this form of question is in controlling the talkative respondent. Summary questions serve to prevent drift away from the purpose of the discussion and allow the questioner to regain control smoothly without the necessity for a bald interruption in the form of, 'Now we must get back to …'. There are better ways of doing this, for example by asking the respondent to summarise what they have said:

'Thank you – that was interesting. Now, I wonder if you could summarise what happened after that? I'd like to get the broad picture first and then we can come back to particular points.'

Summary questions are very closely allied to closed questions, which will be considered in Chapter 2.

The value – at work – of open questions

It is important to emphasise that all these forms of open questions have immense value in everyday occurrences at work. As already pointed out, such questions prompt the person being asked really to think through the various issues. The value of having someone else ask us questions is that they may think of some we would never have thought of asking ourselves – or don't want to ask! Others, by listening to our responses, may also hear our own inconsistencies or the gaps in our thinking.

Staff who have experienced such good questioning – which is both supportive and challenging, because done in the right tone of voice (ie not aggressively) – report that they subsequently feel able to take on more responsibilities: they feel more confident about tackling and resolving issues simply because they know how to ask *themselves* more probing questions. And if they feel stuck, they will ask colleagues to help them by means of questions.

This way, everyone learns what the good questions are that lead to an exploration and opening-up of new avenues. Managers of people who have learnt to ask questions find, of course, that they have to be prepared either to answer or to discuss openly with staff, and to respond to them. But the bonus is that staff tend to come to them armed with ideas rather than with the 'What shall we do about ...?' type of question.

Passive questioning

Passive questioning is not, strictly speaking, passive, for the questioner (who of course is also the listener) is showing that he is listening to responses and, rather than interrupt the flow with words, is signalling interest, support, and encouragement. We show this more passive form of questioning in a variety of ways.

Non-verbal encouragement

Non-verbal encouragement is one way of letting the respondent know that the other person is listening to what they are saying and, more than that, is sufficiently interested to hear more. Encouraging noises such has 'aha', 'mm', 'oh' are indications of attention; together with appropriate facial expressions (smiles, raised eyebrows, etc) head movements and body posture, they encourage the respondent to continue talking. This often precludes the need for supplementary questions because the extended response to the non-verbal noises will have covered points the questioner would have raised.

Supportive comments/link questions

Supportive comments and link questions are the verbal equivalent of non-verbal encouragement. Phrases like 'I see ...', 'That's interesting ...', 'And then?' or 'And what happened next?' are merely different ways of saying, 'Go on,

I'm with you – tell me more.' Used sensitively, such expressions will produce the same results as non-verbal noises – an extended answer which may reduce the need for further questions.

Key word repetition

Key word repetition is a further way in which a respondent can be encouraged to say more. If the questioner is doing their job properly (not only asking the right questions, but also concentrating on the responses) it will not be difficult to pick out particular words or phrases with which to respond. For example:

'For two years I've been working in the research department, concentrating on tribology.'

'Oh …, tribology …?'

When asked with a questioning inflection, this will normally be sufficient to encourage the respondent to explain in more detail what they have been doing, leaving the interviewer in no doubt as to what tribology involves, even if they had previously assumed that it must be something to do with the study of primitive peoples!

Mirror questions

Sometimes known as the 'reverse' question, the mirror question adopts the same approach. If the respondent has given a short answer and the interviewer wants to know more, they merely rephrase the response as a question.

For example, part of an interview attempting to establish the reasons for an employee's resignation might go something like this:

'I couldn't work with that particular supervisor'

'You couldn't work with that particular supervisor?'

'No, he was always getting at me.'

'He was always getting at you?'

'Yes, it made me nervous.'

'It made you nervous?' etc

Even this short extract is sufficient to show the biggest shortcoming of this question form. In the hands of a novice questioner it can be used too much! It can even become irritating.

On the other hand, both the key word repetition and mirror questions are approaches favoured by VIPs when making conversation with lesser mortals. A fragment of such a conversation might go something like this:

'And what do *you* do for a living?'

'Oh, I'm an engineer.'

'An engineer?'

'Yes, I build bridges.'

'You build bridges?'

'Yes, I'm responsible for making sure that …' and so forth.

Neither the key word repetition nor the mirror should be overused, but they are useful ways of extracting further information. Such approaches can prove highly informative as long as the respondent is basically willing to talk. Most people are, but there are occasions when a slightly different approach is required to get the conversation flowing:

'And what do *you* do for a living?'

'Oh, I'm an engineer.'

'An engineer?'

'Yes.'

'What does that involve?' (open question)

'Well …, I'm responsible for making sure that …' and so forth.

It is obvious that the questioner would have made increasingly heavy weather of the conversation if he had not fallen back on an open question to broaden the topic.

The pause
Too many people feel that they need to fill silences. Yet silences most often indicate that the person is thinking about his or her response. There is no reason why a respondent

should leap in instantly after a question has been asked. In fact, stopping to think will result in a more thought-out and reasoned response.

By remaining silent the questioner shows he is 'with' the respondent. Of course some pauses can become long silences, and then the questioner may need to gauge what is happening. One way is to make a short statement about the silence – maybe by asking the respondent if he or she wants more time, or whether something in unclear, or simply whether they need more time to think. Body language will also give clues about how the respondent is feeling.

If the questioner wants the respondent to add to what he has already said, a pause can indicate that more is expected just as effectively as would a spoken question. Remember Mark Twain's advice: 'The right word may be effective but no word was ever as effective as a rightly timed pause'!

Obviously, during the pause the other person should not be totally immobile and fix the respondent with an unrelenting stare (although this is a posture adopted by some parents when dragging a story out of an unwilling child!). A mixture of non-verbal noises and head-nodding, whilst fixing the eye on some neutral point, followed by an enquiring glance at the respondent, can all indicate that the response has evoked deep thought. Depending on the respondent's perception, the questioner's reaction may be interpreted in a variety of ways. For example:

'Very interesting …. Yes, I'd certainly like to hear more.'

'I'm not sure I'm with you …. Could you go through that again? … I do want to be sure I really understand what you're saying, don't I?'

Such pauses become pregnant only if the respondent feels he has said all he has to say on the matter and is waiting for the other person to say something. If this doesn't happen each will continue waiting for the other, obviously with confused results.

2 closed questioning

The purpose of the closed (or 'restrictive' or 'direct') question is to supply the questioner with specific items of information. The respondent is severely restricted in their reply and has little chance to develop their thoughts. As a result it requires very little effort from them, and correspondingly more from the questioner. (It is a little like a game of tennis where the ball seems to be in the server's court virtually all the time.)

This form of question may be overused by unskilled interviewers, not least because such questions are easy to phrase and are apparently time-saving. In the past much advice has been given to novice interviewers about not using closed questions. However, such questions are helpful principally in verifying information, and also in redirecting an interview back towards its purpose, or even emphasising a vital point. There are two main categories of closed questions, as shown below.

Forms of closed questions

Question form	Purpose
Yes/No response Identification	To establish specific facts/information

Yes/No response

Any question phrased to produce either a 'yes' or 'no' answer has severely limited use in an interview. If its use is confined to confirming items of interest or seeking specific answers, it can be valuable.

For instance, a doctor relies heavily on the yes/no response during diagnosis of some health problems.

'Now, ... if I press there does that hurt?'

'No.'

'Or there?'

'No.' .

'What about here?'

'No.'

'Or here?'

'Ye-e-s!'

In other situations, however, the use of this type of question may cause real headaches. To take an example from an interview for a job, a novice interviewer should be wary of starting any such question with 'I see that ...?' whilst concentrating on his paperwork. Lack of preparation for the interview soon shows through!

'I see that you were at school in Doncaster?'

'Yes.'

'And I see you took A-levels in Economics and Geography?'

'Yes.'

'And went on from there to college to read philosophy?'

'No – I worked abroad for a year first.'

'Oh ... er ... yes ... I see ... I'm sorry.'

The unintentional use of a closed question can often be overcome by a simple expedient – following it with a simple interrogative probe. For example:

'Do you feel that was the right thing to do?'

'Yes, I do.'

'Why?'

'Are you concerned about the present situation?'

'Yes, I am.'

'Why?' or 'What concerns you in particular?'

'Did you keep the appointment last week?'

'No.'

'Why not?' or 'What stopped you?'

This approach can also prove particularly effective when dealing with evasive responses to open questions. The questioner closes the dialogue right down to force a definite response. They are then in a position to explore the reasoning behind the response by asking a simple interrogative probe.

A trap for a questioner who asks closed questions is an overeagerness to help. For instance, the question 'Why did you decide to do that?… Was it because …?' illustrates the point. The 'why' part of the question stands perfectly well on its own because it is impossible to answer with a simple 'yes' or 'no'. Such prompting develops into a form of 'leading' questions – which are counter-productive (see page 41).

Fact-seeking questions

Some questions that start with 'Who?' 'Where?' 'When?' 'How many?' etc are fact-seeking questions, because they seek to identify a person, a place, a time, or a number. They are closed questions even though they cannot be answered by a simple 'yes' or 'no'. For example:

'How many people do you have reporting to you?'

'How long did that job take you?'

'What were your best subjects at school?'

'When will you be able to deliver the books?'

'How many children do you have?'

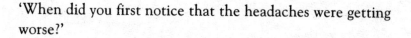

'When did you first notice that the headaches were getting worse?'

The only possible answers to such questions are direct and specific. Consider the following list of 'identification' questions; there is one on the list that is out of place. Having identified it, what sort of question would you say it is?

'What is your name?'

'What is your date of birth?'

'Where were you born?'

'What is your address?'

'How long have you lived there?'

'How do you like living there?'

'Where did you live previously?'

The usefulness of fact-seeking questions should not be underestimated – any fact-finding question can be a valuable tool if used wisely. They can also be very helpful, for instance, when used by colleagues to help one another resolve problems. For instance:

'Whom did you talk to?'

'Was he helpful?'

'Have you considered asking someone else?'

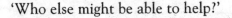

'Who else might be able to help?'

Although ostensibly 'closed', these questions in fact help to open a respondent's mind (see Extension and precision questions on page 16). (For an example of the sort of closed 'identification' and related open and probe questions used by managers in performing their jobs see Appendix 3.)

3 counter-productive questioning

Any question that plainly detracts from or undermines the purpose of asking it is a counter-productive question. Any question that suggests the 'right' answer, confuses or misleads the respondent, prevents talking or discourages them is counter-productive, and should be avoided at all times.

Forms of counter-productive questions

Question form	Purpose
Leading	To prompt desired answer
Trick	To confuse or mislead
Multiple	
Marathon	
Ambiguous	
Rhetorical	To prevent respondent from saying anything
Discriminatory	To discourage respondent/indicate bias

Leading questions

Any devotee of court-room dramas on television will be familiar with the leading question. Sometimes known as a 'loaded' or 'provocative' question, its purpose is quite clear:

to prompt the desired answer. Put more formally, the leading question contains within its form the expected answer, which is itself an assumption on the part of the questioner. In other words, the leading question is suggestive – it suggests the right answer, the one the questioner expects. It puts words into the mouth of the respondent and this is precisely why it should not be used.

The leading *statement*, on the other hand, relies for its effect on the unspoken request for agreement. The neighbour who greets you with the statement 'Lovely day!' is inviting agreement, even though the 'Isn't it?' is unspoken. It is just another way of putting words into the respondent's mouth. We use leading statements like this all the time in everyday conversation, but such statements are much less acceptable during, say, an interview. An example of a frequently quoted and obviously leading question – 'How many times last week did you beat your wife?' – is sufficient to show the dangers inherent in this approach! The questioner is really saying 'Look, I know already that you beat your wife – all I'm interested in is establishing precisely how many times last week you actually did so.'

The main point to remember is that any lead, other than the conversational, is potentially dangerous because of its provocative nature. Assertions like 'I take it you believe that...?' 'You've got to admit that...?' and 'Isn't it a fact that...?' may produce an overreaction in terms of 'No, I don't!' or 'It most certainly is *not* a fact.' A critical lead (see page 46) may have the same effect. The question 'You don't *really* think that… do you?', itself a provocative contradiction, could be the unwitting prelude to a heated argument rather than a rational discussion.

Some variations of the leading question are given in the following sections.

The straightforward lead

This question form is usually phrased in terms of a clear emotional appeal, which is why it is sometimes called an 'obvious' question. The straightforward lead begins with phrases like:

'You've got to admit that…?'

'Isn't it a fact that…?'

'You must concede that…?'

'You will acknowledge…?'

'You cannot deny that…?'

'You wouldn't say that…?'

'You don't think that…?'

'You're not suggesting that…?'

Each is designed to produce a definite 'right' answer. In the case of the first group of examples above, the questioner is expecting the answer 'Yes, of course!' In the second group of questions, the suggested and obviously appropriate answer is 'No, of course not.' In every case the questioner's appeal is 'Please tell me what I want to hear – I'm making it as easy as I can for you.'

There are many more examples of straightforward leads. For example, one question sometimes asked of applicants for jobs is, 'You will be able to cope, won't you?' Who in their right mind would answer 'no' to that?

As you read each of the following questions, consider the answers you are being led to give.

1   'I presume you're confident you can do the job?'

2   'Your knowledge is up to date, I suppose?'

3   'You are trustworthy, aren't you?'

4   'Your timekeeping is OK, I take it?'

5   'We can't afford mistakes in Accounts. Your figure work is accurate, I suppose?'

6   'Most qualified people think that…. What is your view?'

7   'Informed opinion within our profession is that…. What do you think?'

8   'It's absolutely vital that the successful candidate gets on well with the members of the team already appointed. How do you get on with people, generally speaking?'

In each case, the expected answer has already been telegraphed to the respondent. To take the first five examples above, is there really any other answer apart from 'Of course'? Also, in questions (6) and (7), the pressure to agree with the views of 'qualified people' and 'informed opinion' is considerable. (Next time you watch a television interview, see how many times this type of lead is used and judge whether the respondent deals with it effectively.) The last question, question (8), is not a lead as such. However, the opening statement is sufficient to suggest the acceptable answer, even though the question itself is seeking an opinion. How many respondents are going to admit that they do not get on with people?

In seeking to avoid closed questions it's easy to fall into the obvious trap of leading questions.

A few examples are sufficient to show just how easy this is.

'Do you have a job now?' (Closed question)

'You do have a job now, don't you?' (Lead)

'Are you coming to the football match?' (Closed question)

'You are coming to the football match, aren't you?' (Lead)

'Have you renewed your licence?' (Closed question)

'You have renewed your licence, haven't you?' (Lead)

'Do you use leading questions when interviewing?' (Closed question)

'You don't really use leading questions when interviewing, do you?' (Lead)

A further word of caution: even when asking a closed question such as 'Do you use leading questions when interviewing?' voice inflection alone can give a very positive lead as to the expected answer. (Try saying the question out loud, and stress the word 'you'. The lead is there even without a shaking of the head!)

Even without using any particular inflection, the person asking the question can influence its reception. A smooth 'Is that a good place to leave your car, sir?', when asked by a police officer, can change what is a closed question into a definite lead!

The critical lead

This variation of the leading question relies for its effect on a minimum of implied sarcasm.

'Surely you can't believe that…, can you?'

'You don't really think that…, do you?'

'Surely you're not suggesting that…?'

'You don't honestly think that…, do you?'

'Do you really suppose…?'

The critical lead has an emotional appeal similar to that contained in the straightforward lead, but the emotion is rather more pointed. Anything less than a vehement denial of the content of the question appears to imply a lack of intelligence, or even irrationality. How many respondents are going to take these suggestions lightly?

The highly charged emotional nature of the critical lead can produce a strong reaction in an unsuspecting respondent. This is why it is used where the intention is to unsettle the respondent in order to gauge his or her reaction. (This is sometimes referred to as 'stress questioning or interviewing'.)

The reverse lead

An interesting variation on the straightforward leading question is what may be called the 'reverse' lead. The reverse lead occurs when a *respondent* answers a question with another question. This approach can unsettle some people and restrict the smooth flow of conversation unless handled with a deft touch.

The following fragment from the start of a grievance interview is one example:

Question: 'What can I do to help?'

Answer: 'Plenty – my overtime payment has been forgotten, hasn't it? And my pay-slip is short, isn't it?'

Reverse leads are often used in other contexts; for example:

Question: 'What were you doing?'

Answer: 'I was just minding my own business, wasn't I?'

Question: 'Can you tell me why you left your last job?'

Answer: 'Well, it's obvious, isn't it? I didn't get on with the boss, did I?'

Question: 'Can you tell me what the problem is?'

Answer: 'Well, I keep getting this pain. Know what I mean?'

Each answer is a simple request for agreement. Most questioners would recognise these answers for what they are and sidestep the suggested response without any trouble. But if such reverse leads are not immediately identified, the questioner may feel forced into prefacing each succeeding question with 'Yes, but...?' unless they remember to use a 'mirror' or 'key word repetition' to regain control, for example:

'Just minding your own business...?'

'Didn't get on...?'

'Pain...?'

Offer of alternatives

The use of a simple question such as 'Are you married or single?' is sufficient to show the obvious shortcomings of this particular type of lead. The questioner is really saying: 'I'd like to establish your marital status. You've got to be either married or single – now , which is it?' This question does not allow for other (unrecognised) possibilities – widowed, separated, divorced, or co-habiting.

The 'offer of alternatives' is quite simply an offer of 'either-or': either the answer is this or it is that. The questioner's assumption is that there are only two possible answers, both of which are incorporated in the question. Another example illustrates this point:

'Do you think that attitude or skill is the most important factor in this situation?'

But what about knowledge? The respondent may well feel that this factor is far more important than either of the alternatives offered by the questioner. One more example:

'Did you find that particular experience useful, or was it a waste of time?'

Again, the respondent may feel that a truthful answer would lie somewhere between these two extremes.

A variation on the simple offer of two alternatives is what has been called the 'laundry-list' or 'shop-window' question. This type offers a range of possible answers. It is still a leading question, because the questioner is putting a choice of possible 'right' answers on display and inviting the respondent to make a choice:

'What do you think is the most important quality needed for this job? Is it dependability, conscientiousness, ability to get on with people, loyalty, perseverance, or capacity for hard work, do you think?'

This type of question may be helpful if the respondent seems to be suffering from a temporary mental blockage and needs help to channel their thoughts in the right direction. However, it does require the addition of two or three more words at the end of the question to show that the answer need not be confined to the possibilities offered. The words are 'or what?', or 'or something else?'

'What do you think the top priority of a production supervisor should be? (Pause)… (Recognition of mental blockage)… Should it be to minimise wastage, keep his people happy, maintain quality standards… or what?'

The addition of the 'or what?' neatly changes the thrust of the question from a lead to an opinion-seeking question. Even in this form, however, it should be used sparingly and only when absolutely necessary to prevent the 'conversation' becoming nothing more than the completion of a verbal questionnaire.

The complex lead

As the name indicates, the difference between a straightforward lead and a complex lead lies in the degree of complexity in the subject matter. The complex lead takes a subject about which the respondent may know little or nothing and assumes specialist and detailed knowledge. The 'right' answer may still be a brief 'yes' or 'no', although it will probably include a further justification of the reply.

Consider the following questions:

'Something pretty drastic has obviously got to be done about international exchange rates, hasn't it?'

'It seems that the recent change in base rate and the subsequent action by the Association are certainly going to make endowment policies more attractive, aren't they?'

'Budget cutbacks in the public sector will mean that much more effort will have to be made to provide the sort of service we can be proud of, won't it?'

Each of these complex leads assumes specialist knowledge and begs for a 'yes' answer. Some questioners use this question form to test the depth of a respondent's understanding of a particular subject. However, such leads can easily be reversed by a skilled respondent using a 'key word repetition':

'Pretty drastic...?'

'More attractive...?'

'More effort...?'

If only on this basis, a complex lead should not be used because it is confusing: does the questioner want a reply? And if the 'question' contains several statements, which one should be replied to? It is much better to frame the question as an open or probe question to test knowledge. For instance, a neutral 'What do you think will be the effect of budget cutbacks on the service we provide?' is likely to be much more effective in prompting a full answer from the respondent.

Complex leads should be avoided. Apart from anything else, they border on the rhetorical (see below). A thoughtful silence on the part of the respondent is usually sufficient to persuade the questioner to launch into a lengthy justification of the original premiss!

The personal lead

It is one thing to ask, even unwittingly, a leading question on a neutral topic such as international exchange rates, and it is quite another to be provocative at a very personal level. The crux of a personal lead is that it assumes the existence of a negative personality trait. Even having said that, however, some personal leads seem much more acceptable than others, for example:

'When did you last lose your temper?'

The questioner is really saying 'Look, *everybody* loses their temper at some time or another. Just tell me the last time you lost yours.' There are few people who would find such a question unacceptable, because it is generally agreed that losing your temper is a fact of life, however infrequently it may occur.

There are other personal leads, however, that are likely to be much less acceptable and may provoke a hostile reaction. For example:

'From what you've just been saying, you do seem to let your emotions colour your judgement, don't you?'

'How do you cope with life's problems when you are feeling inadequate?'

'When was the last time you really failed at something – you know... dropped an almighty clanger?'

'What sort of things make you particularly nervous?'

'Would you say you were a particularly obstinate sort of person?'

'When was the last time you let somebody down?'

'Do you feel like kicking over the traces very often?'

'That really was a stupid thing to do, wasn't it?'

'How often do you feel aggressive?'

In every case the questioner is assuming the existence of a negative personality trait – 'inadequacy', 'failure', 'nervousness', 'obstinacy', 'aggression', 'stupidity' etc. These words are all examples of what other people are like, never what we are like ourselves! Consider your own reaction to being labelled with any one of them. How would you feel? Even for a normally mild-mannered person the assumption of a negative trait, aggression for instance, could easily become a self-fulfilling prophecy.

Multiple and marathon questions

This type of question consists of a number of closed questions presented as a package to an increasingly bemused respondent:

'You did say you wouldn't mind being away from home occasionally? Oh, and you do have a current driving licence, don't you? I presume it's clean? And, er, by the way…?' etc, etc.

The response to such a rapid-fire approach is confused. The respondent may try to digest the questions and order his answers mentally whilst desperately trying to remember the first question in the series – all this as the interviewer finally finishes and sits back expectantly. There are few respondents who have the concentration, confidence and aplomb to answer, 'I did, I do and it is' – an answer which is itself likely to make the questioner squirm!

These multiple and marathon questions are often strung together by people who feel a great deal of enthusiasm and energy – and sometimes by those who are really worried and stressed about something. The questions often emerge like shots from an automatic machine-gun. But such questions are also used by people who don't expect an answer, and are using this formula to express their own thoughts. A potential respondent then turns into a mere listener. (See Rhetorical questions overleaf.)

Ambiguous questions

Some questions may leave a respondent confused. The source of the confusion is usually the ambiguous phrasing of the question itself.

An example of such a question, meaningless in itself, is 'What about religion?' The likely mental reaction – or even actual response – of anyone who has been subjected to other forms of counter-productive questions previously is, 'Well, what about it? What do you want me to say?'

Ambiguous questions that have this effect include:

'What's London like?'

'Are you a people person?'

'What are you like with women (or men!)?'

When interviewers indulge in such questions, interviewees emerge muttering about incompetence and stupidity. The outcome will be damage to the interviewer's reputation and that of the organisation he represents. It is worth remembering that it is the questioner who controls the interview. Asking an ambiguous question inevitably results in loss of control.

When a colleague or manager asks such an ambiguous question, it may be an invitation simply to begin talking and see where the discussion goes. But even then, the person being posed such a question would do well to ask, 'What exactly do you mean?' or state, 'I don't understand your question.'

Rhetorical questions

Rhetorical questions are the ones that the questioner asks but doesn't expect to be answered; he answers them himself. The word 'rhetoric' really says it all: 'the art of using language to persuade or influence others.' It's a way of leading on to, or introducing, points a speaker wants to make. So: 'Do we really want…? No, of course we don't. It would mean…' Or: 'and how has it come about that…? We all know, don't we, that…?'

You probably begin to recognise the formula. It's used frequently by politicians and other public speakers.

Discriminatory questions

Discriminatory questions are asked only of certain categories of people: women, racial or religious minorities, the old, the disabled, or even the young. They are often based on a stereotype, a false assumption, or bias held by the questioner.

Three of the categories mentioned above are protected in law from discrimination: women, racial 'minorities', and the disabled. In other words, asking discriminatory questions of such people could result in the questioner being summoned to a tribunal. Legislation does not, however, protect the young, or prohibit discrimination on grounds of religious persuasion or sexual orientation.

Discriminatory questions can often arise in a job interview, and so the examples that follow will focus on this situation. When someone is holding an interview for a job, the only valid questions they may ask will relate to the candidate's knowledge, skills, abilities, and willingness to do the job concerned. Nonetheless, discriminatory questions do arise, especially when people who have not traditionally done a certain type of job apply for it.

In job interviews it could be discriminatory to ask:

● men or women if they are married

■ women if they plan to have children (especially if men are not asked)

▲ women how they plan to cope with school holidays

◉ black people how they expect to cope with white customers

◉ a Muslim or a Jew if they go to their place of worship on a Friday or Saturday.

These questions have nothing to do with an applicant's ability to do a job. Since the passing of laws on discrimination such questioning occurs less and less. But it can pose problems for both questioner and respondent. Anyone involved in conducting job interviews should read the specialised literature on recruitment interviewing and discrimination.

Expecting answers?

We have already seen that many questioners:

◉ don't expect answers, ie they ask rhetorical questions

◼ ask questions and go on to provide 'leading' answers

▲ expect answers but don't give the listener enough time to formulate them

◉ interrupt respondents half-way through their answer.

To test out whether you expect, and listen to, the answers to your questions, think about the questions you ask in everyday life and consider how often you find yourself showing the following characteristics. Please tick the appropriate box in each case. The scoring table for this questionnaire is shown on page 63.

CHARACTERISTIC	FREQUENCY				
	ALMOST NEVER	OFTEN	SOME- TIMES	SELDOM	ALMOST ALWAYS
1 Being clear about why you are using a particular type of question					
2 'Seeing' your questions from the other person's point of view					
3 Encouraging a speaker to continue without saying anything yourself					
4 Interrupting answers to your questions with 'yes but...'					
5 Signalling the response you want					
6 Answering your own questions					
7 Finishing speakers' sentences for them					
8 Not asking questions which you think may show your ignorance					
9 Letting your mind wander and mishearing replies					
10 Needing to repeat your questions					

Background to the questions

QUESTION 1	Many people have never thought about the various types of question open to them. It's assumed that because we can speak, we can therefore ask questions. At a simple level this is true. However, being absolutely clear about why we are asking particular questions and knowing how to phrase them effectively is a positive skill which can be developed with practice.
2	Much of the skill associated with phrasing questions effectively is based on assessing accurately how someone may react. Even a humorous question asked in an aggressive or overassertive manner may provoke a similar response! It is worth remembering that people respond in terms of what they think you are saying, which will be hidden behind, and between, the words you actually use. Even a simple enquiry may be perceived indirectly as a criticism! For example, take the simple question, 'What time did you get in last night?' What is the questioner implying?
3	Pausing when someone has finished replying to a question to allow a further response is one of the marks of the truly effective questioner. Too many people jump in immediately with another question. It is worth remembering that people sometimes need time to clarify and gather their thoughts as they are speaking. Pausing allows them to do just this. Consider the following comment about a famous TV interviewer: 'The great thing about [Alan] Whicker is that he's bright enough not to chip in immediately you've finished talking. He always waits. So you feel obliged to say a bit more. And before you know it, you've said far more than you ever intended.'

4 An all-too-common tendency is to 'butt-in' in the middle of a response. The skilled questioner/listener avoids interrupting with 'yes, but …' and invariably encourages the speaker to continue. Such an approach takes courage: it does involve the risk of being influenced by another's thinking! The old saying 'Don't confuse me with your ideas, I've already made up my mind' applies to each of us perhaps more than we may care to admit.

If you think these remarks cannot possibly apply to you, check over the next week how many times you use the words 'yes, but…'!

5 Many people use leading questions without being aware that they are doing so. Putting words into somebody's mouth in general conversation is perhaps acceptable but in other settings, for instance at work, can be rather off-putting. The use of leading questions should be restricted unless you really do wish to force someone into a corner. And could you handle the counter-attack?

6 Answering your own questions can be very irritating for other people. Certainly politicians (and salesmen!) use rhetorical questions to pose the issues they feel ought to be considered. In most other situations such predictions about facts, emotions and attitudes tend to be resented by more independent spirits, and this resentment will burst through sooner or later. The use of rhetorical questions is not recommended.

7 To finish the sentences of someone with whom you are holding a conversation is another irritating mannerism which can easily be avoided. It is not only discourteous but presumes that you are in possession of a particularly accurate crystal ball!

QUESTION **8**	Asking questions is not about showing up your ignorance, although there is no reason why you should know, or be expected to know, everything. Asking a question is usually a genuine request for clarification; and there is nothing wrong with wanting to clarify matters. Besides, you'll find that the question you ask is often one that others also want to ask, but don't have the courage to!
9	At one level, concentrating on the reply when you have asked a question is nothing more than common courtesy to the speaker. But, your mind can accommodate 500 – 600 words a minute, whereas most people speak at only 120 – 130 words a minute. In other words your 'thought-rate' is much superior to normal 'speech-rate'. So the effective questioner/listener is sifting the evidence and evaluating what is being said, while also continuing to listen.
10	Some questioners are prone to ask questions that rely for their impact on technical jargon. It has been estimated that there are over 300,000 technical terms in the English language, and no matter how many you know they still represent a small portion of the total. How can you be sure that the terms you know and use will be precisely the same ones others know and use? This is perfectly acceptable between experts who talk the same special language but can be a major stumbling-block for people who are not only unfamiliar with this language but who also do not wish, for whatever reason, to show their ignorance. Others ask questions that are ill thought-out and badly worded, and this may be why they are asked to repeat the question! (It might be interesting now to reflect on your responses to questions 3 and 8.)

Scoring your responses

Shown below are the scores for the questionnaire. (To persuade you to complete the questionnaire first before you look at the table, it is presented upside down!)

QUESTION NUMBER	ALMOST ALWAYS	OFTEN	SOME-TIMES	SELDOM	ALMOST NEVER
1	10	8	6	4	2
2	10	8	6	4	2
3	10	8	6	4	2
4	2	4	6	8	10
5	2	4	6	8	10
6	2	4	6	8	10
7	2	4	6	8	10
8	2	4	6	8	10
9	2	4	6	8	10
10	2	4	6	8	10

Even if your score is in the eighties, or more, it is still probable that you could extend your skills in this direction. At the back of this book are some suggestions for further reading which may help to start the process.

4 summary

1   Be clear about the purpose of your questions before you ask them. Concentrate on using open questions; they produce greater results.

Question Type	Purpose	Question Form	Illustrations
OPEN	To establish rapport	Contact	Introductory questions/comments to establish the first superficial relationship and to put respondent at ease, eg in a selection interview or at a first meeting.
	To show interest/encouragement	Non-verbal encouragement	Umm? Er? Ah? Oh? Hmm? together with appropriate facial expressions (smiles, raised eyebrows) and head movements.
		Supportive statements	'I see ...? 'And then ...? 'That's interesting ...? (ie tell me more).
		Key word repetition	Repetition of one or two words to encourage further response.
		Mirror	Repetition of short reply as a query.
		The pause	Allied to various non-verbal signals.

Question Type	Purpose	Question Form	Illustrations
OPEN (cont)	To seek further information	Simple interrogative	'Why?' 'Why not?'
		Comparative	'How do your responsibilities now compare with those in your last job?'
		Extension and precision	'How do you mean?' 'What makes you say that?'
		Hypothetical	'What would you do if ...?' 'How would you feel if ...?'
	To explore in detail particular opinions/ attitudes	Opinion-seeking	'How do you feel about ...?' 'What do you think about ...?' 'To what extent do you feel ...?' 'Just how far do you think ...?'
		The reflection	'You think that ...?' 'It seems to you that ...?' 'You feel that ...?'
	To demonstrate understanding/ clarify information already given	Summary	'As I understand it ...?' 'If I've got it right ...?' 'So what you're saying is ...?'
CLOSED	To establish specific facts/ information	Yes/No response	'Are you ...?' 'Do you ...?' 'Have you ...?'
		Identification of person, time, location, number	'How many people do you have reporting to you ...?' 'How long did you have that job?'

Use link questions to move smoothly from one type of question to another, eg 'You mentioned just now that... How did this affect your work?' 'You were saying earlier that... What happened after that?'

2   Do not use counter-productive questions: the aim is to
    get the respondent talking, not to suggest 'right' answers;
    embarrass, confuse or mislead him; prevent him from
    saying anything; or discourage him.

Question Type	Purpose	Question Form	Illustrations
COUNTER-PRODUCTIVE	To prompt desired answer	Leading	'I take it you believe that …?' 'You don't *really* think that … do you?' 'You must admit that …?' 'Isn't it a fact that …?'
	To confuse or mislead	Multiple and Marathon	Two or more questions presented as a package. 'You did say you wouldn't mind being away from home occasionally? Oh, and you do have a current driving licence, don't you? I presume it's clean? And, er, by the way …?' etc.
			Asking a question in a rambling, incomprehensible way.
		Ambiguous	'What about religion?'
	To prevent respondent from saying anything	Rhetorical	Answering your own questions. 'Do you …? Of course you do. I always say that … etc.'
	To discourage respondent/ indicate bias	Discriminatory	'When do you intend to start a family?'

3   Remember that even with your mouth firmly shut, you
    will still be communicating, whether you like it or not.
    The expression on your face together with your head

movements and the way you are sitting are positive signals for the respondent just as much as the questions you ask and the way in which you ask them.

Consider the following diagram and assess the image you habitually project in interview situations. Could it be improved?

Sympathetic gestures	Aggressive posture
Proximity	
Relaxed tone of voice	Harsh tone of voice
Smiles	'Set' mouth
'Crinkled' eyes	Distance
Expansive gestures	Staring eyes

Warmth signified by | Hostility signified by

Non-verbal communications

Control/ domination signified by | Submissiveness signified by

Speaking loudly/ quickly all the time	Speaking quietly/ saying little
Ignoring responses	Allowing interruptions
Interrupting	Meek tone of voice
'Controlling' tone of voice	Downcast eyes
'Stabbing' fingers and other forceful gestures	'Handwashing' and other nervous gestures

Check-list

● Keep your objectives clearly in mind.

■ Establish a pattern of questioning that can be followed.

○ Within this pattern ask open questions.

□ Restrict the use of closed questions.

△ Don't ask counter-productive questions.

▲ Use plain language.

● Allow thinking time for response.

● Analyse replies.

○ What does the respondent *seem* to be trying to communicate?

□ What can be inferred from the way he or she communicates and the words he or she uses?

△ What does he or she convey by his or her approach to the subject?

● Observe and interpret the details of the respondent's non-verbal signals (gestures, facial expressions, movement of limbs, blinking, coughing etc) which can reveal his or her emotional state.

■ Maintain an atmosphere of friendly neutrality: remember your own non-verbal signals!

▲ Don't talk too much.

LISTEN – OBSERVE – ANALYSE

appendices

Appendix 1 Developing a training session on question technique

Most trainers would prefer to develop their own course material if they had the time to do so. For those who cannot spare the time, the following outline for a session on asking questions is put forward as one possible approach. It is based on the training principle of moving from the known to the unknown. Because driving a car is an everyday occurrence for many people, it makes a useful analogy for developing a discussion of question technique.

Questioning technique. In any purposeful conversation a variety of questions will be used, interspersed with other forms of communicating. Below are some of the variations.

1 Steering. To reach its objective, the conversation must be steered in the required direction. To do this a questioner needs to concentrate on three things:

(a) Listening: not just hearing the replies to questions but positively listening to the answers as a basis for carrying the conversation forward.

(b) Analysing: this means thinking in some detail about the answers. What is the respondent really saying? How is it being said? What of importance is *not* being said?

(c) Observing: the whole manner of approach of the respondent should be noted. Accurate assessment of non-verbal communication is as important as evaluation of the verbal responses.

2 Use of Gears. The speed of the vehicle depends on the use of various gears. In this context closed questions of the yes/no type are the equivalent of first and second gears. Questions which produce yes/no answers will take the conversation forward but only very slowly. It is definitely uphill work for the questioner.

Consider how long it would take the average driver to reach his destination if he was restricted exclusively to using these low gears. Think of the wear and tear on the car, to say nothing of the effect on the driver's equanimity! So closed questions – like first and second gears – should be used only when absolutely necessary.

Open questions are the equivalent of third gear. Such questions give the questioner a degree of flexibility not possible with closed questions. There is time for the questioner to concentrate much more on listening and analysing responses and observing the respondent's behaviour. This, in turn, will assist a more speedy achievement of the overall aim. In other words, the conversation will reach its destination a bit more quickly.

But to move towards the objective at the greatest speed possible, fourth gear – or probing questions – are necessary. Such probes are designed to seek further detailed information and explore opinions/attitudes in detail.

On the other hand, reverse gear – or counter-productive questions – will have precisely the opposite effect. The use of any form of counter-productive question will increase rather than decrease the distance from the objective and consequently the time taken to reach it. At no point during an interview should you be going backwards!

3 The Clutch. The clutch represents link questions. The use of these questions allows the questioner to make a smooth change from one type of question to another.

4 The Accelerator. The proper use of the gears and clutch moves the vehicle forward. So does the accelerator which, in this context, is represented by the non-verbal encouragement and supportive statements used by the questioner. The use of these approaches helps the conversation to move faster.

5 The Footbrake. The footbrake will however slow the vehicle down. The conversation can be slowed right down, even brought to a halt, by the inadvertent use of any of the following:

- talking down to the respondent

■ talking too much

▲ interrupting

● criticising

● displaying an obvious lack of interest in what the respondent is saying.

6 The Driving Mirror. Another point: many drivers make only infrequent use of the driving mirror to see what is behind them. The same applies to questioners. They do not mentally review earlier parts of the conversation as a guide for action. It is difficult to do this whilst listening to answers and thinking ahead to further questions, but such a review is absolutely vital if the interview is to be truly effective.

7 The Handbrake. Most drivers only use the handbrake when they want to prevent a stationary vehicle rolling away on its own. If the handbrake is inadvertently left on when the vehicle starts, sooner or later the linings will burn out and cause real problems. Questioners should beware of:

● the 'Halo' effect; allowing one *good* characteristic on the part of the respondent to influence, disproportionately, the course of the conversation (and the questioner's judgement).

■ the 'Horns' effect: allowing one *bad* characteristic to overinfluence judgement.

▲ stereotyping: having a fixed (and probably incorrect) mental impression of what the respondent 'ought' to be, and how he 'should' respond.

● prejudice: allowing personal likes and dislikes (physical appearance, clothes, accent, etc) to influence the situation.

Finally... Using the controls sensitively will make the difference in performance between that of an occasional weekend driver and an advanced motorist.

Has anyone criticised your driving skill recently? If so, how did you feel? ... Could the same criticism be applied to your skill at interviewing? ... And if this is the case, what do you think you ought to do to improve the situation?

Appendix 2   Using questions in a training context

The use of questions discussed in the text has as much relevance for trainers as for interviewers, managers and colleagues at work. Without a real understanding of question technique a trainer can never be really effective.

No longer is it conventional to think that there are only two types of question – the teaching question and the testing question – which are useful in the learning situation. There is a whole battery of questions that help learning even though the basic division into the two main types still holds good.

Teaching questions have various purposes, amongst them encouraging and clarifying thought, identifying cause-and-effect relationships and generating new ideas. Each of these purposes may be seen either from the perspective of an individual learner or from the perspective of a group. Testing, or checking, whether learning has taken place may again be directed either at the individual or the group. Using questions in a group, however, requires a slightly different approach. This is because the direction of a particular question may be either towards one chosen respondent within the group or towards the group as a whole.

The tables on pages 78 and 79 show this distinction, together with an indication of the aims or purposes of different questions *within the training context*.

Of course, this is by no means an exhaustive examination of all the question forms available to the trainer. Teaching questions cover the whole range of open and probe questions. Even leading questions may be useful to the trainer in making provocative assertions to start a discussion or test knowledge. However, the limitations of the leading question should be accepted. For instance, both the straightforward lead and the reverse lead are question forms much favoured by some over-enthusiastic members of the teaching profession. They are so keen to push on with the course whilst attempting to retain the attention of the participants that they forget the aim of their questions. Looking back on your schooldays, how many times did you hear questions like this:

'Now, I take the chemical solution...yes?...and then I heat it slowly over the burner, don't I? And the result is...isn't it?

'Right...an equilateral triangle has three equal sides...yes?...therefore all sides are equal, aren't they? Yes?'

The old adage 'Tell them; tell them again; and tell them you've told them' should be practised with caution!

Closed questions, too, can be used to good effect in testing understanding; combined with supplementary probing questions they are extremely valuable teaching tools.

As in any other face-to-face encounter, however, the 'question mix' should be sensitively applied. No participant will learn if faced with a barrage of seemingly hostile questions. Remember your aim: overall success depends on the participants' attention and interest. Your skill in asking the right question at the right time is crucial to that success.

Teaching/learning questions

Question Type	Purpose	Question Form	Illustrations	Target
OPEN	To evaluate individual's background knowledge or experience at beginning of learning session. To draw out a shy or timid person	General	'Will you please tell us what experience you've had in dealing with this particular topic?' (ie Tell us about your experience.)	Individual members of the group
	To draw on experience/training of individual member of group	Opinion-seeking	'What do you think about this question?'	
	To provoke thought		'What do you think of the idea of planning maintenance in your department?	
Sometimes called 'control' questions	To stop irrelevant talk of group member		'How does that tie in with the problem we are discussing?'	
	To wake up sleepy or inattentive group member		'In your experience, what are some of the causes of poor co-operation?' (This being the point under discussion.)	
	To break up an aside discussion between two or more group members		'How would you handle that situation?'	

Question Type	Purpose	Question Form	Illustrations	Target
OPEN (cont)	To stimulate group thinking and start discussion		'In your experience, what are some of the reasons why instructions are not clearly understood?'	The group as a whole
	To bring out points of similarity		'What do you think are the similarities between your responsibilities and those of the general manager?'	
	To redirect a question from a group member back to the group		(Restate question) 'What does anybody else think about this one?'	
	To explore opinions		'Some people say that the use of signs does not prevent accidents; what do you think about it?'	

Testing questions

Question Type	Purpose	Question Form	Illustrations	Target
CLOSED	To check that learning has taken place	Identification (What? Where? When? Who?)	'What are the most important points we've mentioned so far?' 'Having completed this operation, what should we do next?' 'What should we do if . . . happens?' 'Who can solve this problem?' 'What is the purpose of this test?'	May be directed at either the group as a whole or a particular individual

Appendix 3 Questioning the constraints on action

	WHAT?	WHERE?	WHEN?
Time	What is the time-scale?	Where will information about the time-scale be available to inform/remind those involved?	When was the time-scale set? When should it be reviewed?
Cost	What is the scheduled cost of deviations and missed deadlines?	Where will the cost be incurred? In what areas?	When will the cost be incurred? At what points on the time-scale?
People	What people are necessary? What mix of skills, knowledge and experience is needed? What is available now?	Where will the people be needed? In what areas specifically?	When will these people be needed?
Physical Resources	What other resources are needed? What are available now?	Where will these other resources be needed?	When will these resources be used?
Legal Imperatives	What legal statutes must be considered?	Where may the statutes apply? In what situations?	When may these statutes be invoked?
Priorities	What are the priorities? What is essential? Desirable?	Where is the demarcation line between absolute priorities and other requirements?	When were the priorities set? When should they be reviewed?
Information	What information is needed? In what form? What is available now?	Where will the information be needed?	When will the information be needed?
Contingencies	What contingencies may arise?	Where may the contingencies occur? Which are the most likely areas?	When may these contingencies arise/occur? For what reasons?

WHY THAT?	WHY THERE?	WHY THEN?
WHY THOSE?		

WHO?	HOW?		
Who decided the time-scale? In consultation with who else? Who will control/review it? Who will be informed of it?	How will information about the time-scale be communicated to those concerned?	**Time**	
Who estimated/defined/itemised the cost? Who will control the cost?	How will it be incurred? How will it be itemised? How will it be controlled?	**Cost**	
Who will be responsible for ensuring that they are available in the right place, at the right time, in the right numbers, with the right training, doing the right work?	How will they be utilised?	**People**	**What is the degree of interdependence between these constraints? What is the mix? If one constraint becomes more/less important – how will this affect the others?**
Who will use them? Who will control their use?	How will the resources be used? How will their use be controlled?	**Physical Resources**	
Who may invoke them? Who will be responsible for ensuring these legal imperatives are met?	How might they be invoked? With what effect? At what cost?	**Legal Imperatives**	
Who decided the priorities? Who will control action in meeting them?	How were the priorities set?	**Priorities**	
Who should present it? To whom? Who should update it?	How should it be presented? How often must it be updated?	**Information**	
Who will recognise their occurrence? Who will make contingency plans? Who will take remedial action? Who will be informed?	How will the resource mix be affected?	**Contin-gencies**	

WHY THAT PERSON? WHY THOSE PEOPLE?   **WHY IN THAT WAY?**

further reading

ADLER A. *Communicating at Work*. London, McGraw-Hill, 1993

BLAKSTAD M. *and* COOPER A. *The Communicating Organisations*. London, Institute of Personnel and Development, 1997

DECKER B. *How to Communicate Effectively*. London, Kogan Page, 1988

HONEY P. *Improve Your People Skills*. 2nd edn. London, Institute of Personnel and Development, 1997

IVEY A. *Managing Face-to-Face Communication*. Bromley, Chartwell-Bratt, 1988

LEEDS D. *Smart Questions for Successful Managers*. London, Piatkus Books, 1987

MACKAY I. *Listening Skills*. 2nd edn. London, Institute of Personnel and Development, 1995

WICKS R.J. *Helping Others*. London, Souvenir Press, 1994

With over 90,000 members, the **Institute of Personnel and Development** is the largest organisation in Europe dealing with the management and development of people. The IPD operates its own publishing unit, producing books and research reports for human resource practitioners, students, and general managers charged with people management responsibilities.

Currently there are over 160 titles covering the full range of personnel and development issues. The books have been commissioned from leading experts in the field and are packed with the latest information and guidance to best practice.

For free copies of the IPD Books Catalogue, please contact the publishing department:

Tel.: 0181-263 3387
Fax: 0181-263 3850
E-mail: publish@ipd.co.uk
Web: http://www.ipd.co.uk

Orders for books should be sent to:

Plymbridge Distributors
Estover
Plymouth
Devon
PL6 7PZ

(Credit card orders) Tel.: 01752 202 301
Fax: 01752 202 333

Upcoming titles in the *Management Shapers* series

Publication: March 1999

Body Language at Work
Adrian Furnham
ISBN 0 85292 771 1

Introducing NLP
Sue Knight
ISBN 0 85292 772 X

Learning for Earning
Eric Parsloe and Caroline Allen
ISBN 0 85292 774 6

Other titles in the *Management Shapers* series

All titles are priced at £5.95 (£5.36 to IPD members)

The Appraisal Discussion

Terry Gillen

Shows you how to make appraisal a productive and motivating experience for all levels of performer. It includes:

- ● assessing performance fairly and accurately

- ■ using feedback to improve performance

- ▲ handling reluctant appraisees and avoiding bias

- ● agreeing future objectives

- ◎ identifying development needs.

1998 96 pages   ISBN 0 85292 751 7

Assertiveness

Terry Gillen

Will help you feel naturally confident, enjoy the respect of others and easily establish productive working relationships, even with 'awkward' people. It covers:

- understanding why you behave as you do and, when that behaviour is counter-productive, knowing what to do about it

- understanding other people better

- keeping your emotions under control

- preventing others' bullying, flattering or manipulating you

- acquiring easy-to-learn techniques that you can use immediately

- developing your personal assertiveness strategy.

1998 96 pages   ISBN 0 85292 769 X

Constructive Feedback

Roland and Frances Bee

Practical advice on when to give feedback, how best to give it, and how to receive and use feedback yourself. It includes:

- using feedback in coaching, training, and team motivation

- distinguishing between criticism and feedback

- 10 tools of giving constructive feedback

- dealing with challenging situations and people.

1998 96 pages   ISBN 0 85292 752 5

The Disciplinary Interview

Alan Fowler

This book will ensure that you adopt the correct procedures, conduct productive interviews and manage the outcome with confidence. It includes:

- understanding the legal implications

- investigating the facts and presenting the management case

- probing the employee's case and diffusing conflict

- distinguishing between conduct and competence

- weighing up the alternatives to dismissal.

1998 96 pages   ISBN 0 85292 753 3

Leadership Skills

John Adair

Will give you confidence and guide and inspire you on your journey from being an effective manager to becoming a leader of excellence. Acknowledged as a world authority on leadership, Adair offers stimulating insights into:

- recognising and developing your leadership qualities

- acquiring the personal authority to give positive direction and the flexibility to embrace change

- acting on the key interacting needs – to achieve your task, build your team, and develop its members

- transforming the core leadership functions such as planning, communicating and motivating into practical skills you can master.

1998 96 pages   ISBN 0 85292 764 9